The First Congregational Churches

T0364299

The First Congregational Churches

New Light on Separatist Congregations in London 1567–81

BY

ALBERT PEEL, M.A., Litt.D., B.Litt.

Editor of *The Seconde Parte of a Register*

CAMBRIDGE
AT THE UNIVERSITY PRESS
1920

CAMBRIDGE
UNIVERSITY PRESS

University Printing House, Cambridge CB2 8BS, United Kingdom

Cambridge University Press is part of the University of Cambridge.

It furthers the University's mission by disseminating knowledge in the pursuit of education, learning and research at the highest international levels of excellence.

www.cambridge.org
Information on this title: www.cambridge.org/9781316633427

First published 1920
First paperback edition 2016

A catalogue record for this publication is available from the British Library

ISBN 978-1-316-63342-7 Paperback

Cambridge University Press has no responsibility for the persistence or accuracy of URLs for external or third-party internet websites referred to in this publication, and does not guarantee that any content on such websites is, or will remain, accurate or appropriate.

PREFACE

THIS booklet deals with one of the most interesting—and one of the most debated—episodes in the history of early Puritanism. I have for many years had in preparation a work on "Elizabethan Puritanism and Separatism," which will endeavour to trace the development of Nonconformity from Elizabeth's accession to the Hampton Court Conference. Other engagements will prevent the appearance of this work for some time, and therefore this brief instalment is now published.

ALBERT PEEL.

GREAT HARWOOD,
  LANCASHIRE.
24 *May*, 1920.

CONTENTS

THE FIRST CONGREGATIONAL CHURCHES

WHEN DID CONGREGATIONALISM EMERGE?

AT what period in Queen Elizabeth's reign did Congregationalism first emerge? When did the divergence between Puritanism and Separatism actually take place? Was the church gathered by Robert Browne and Robert Harrison in Norwich about 1580 the first Congregational Church in this country, or has Richard Fitz's congregation in London a prior claim to that title? These questions have been asked many times, but so far, in spite of much research—by Waddington, Dexter, and Dale in the last generation, and by Dr Powicke and Mr Burrage among living scholars—they have not received decisive answers. Manuscript sources have recently disclosed a few new facts which considerably lighten the gloom that has long covered this corner of Congregationalism's early history. By bringing these facts into relation with the discoveries and deductions of the scholars just mentioned, it is hoped that the sequence of events will become clearer, and that some of the difficulties will disappear.

PREPARATION—ABROAD

The way to Separation in Elizabeth's reign was prepared in the previous reign alike by the experiences of Protestant exiles[1] on the Continent, and by the experiences of some of those who

---

[1] Cf. the characteristic words of Fuller, *Church History* (1868 ed.), II. 373: "For now nonconformity, in the days of King Edward, was conceived; which afterward, in the reign of Queen Mary, (but beyond sea at Frankfort,) was born; which, in the reign of Queen Elizabeth, was nursed and weaned; which, under King James, grew up a young youth or tall stripling; but, towards the end of King Charles's reign, shot up to the full strength and stature of a man, able, not only to cope with, but conquer, the hierarchy, its adversary."

remained in England. The "troubles" at Frankfort[1] brought prominently before all the English refugees, not merely the merits of the Book of Common Prayer and the value of ecclesiastical discipline, but also the larger question of the place of final authority in the church. The quarrel of Thomas Ashley and other members of the congregation with the minister and elders produced a bitter discussion of the problem: "Are the officers of the church (ministers and elders) the ultimate authority, or are the members of the congregation ?" On the stage of Frankfort was played in miniature the drama that was to be witnessed in the homeland in later years, a drama which concluded with the tragic scenes of a king's execution and civil war. In Fuller's words[2]:

" the penknives of that age are grown into swords in ours, and their writings laid the foundations of the fightings now-a-days."

—AND AT HOME.

While the English Protestants abroad were making their contribution to ecclesiastical evolution through " troubles " and strife, some of those left at home were assisting the same process by witness of another kind. They determined not to forsake the assembling of themselves together, no matter what the civil and ecclesiastical authorities might command. They therefore met for worship constantly, in private houses and in ships, in store rooms and in the open fields, as opportunity offered[3]. Thus they became familiar with the idea and practice of worship in buildings that were not consecrated, and by forms that were not legal. When it was evident, a decade later, that the hopes of purer worship that had been entertained were doomed to dis-

---

[1] *A Brieff discours off the troubles begonne at Franckford in Germany...*, 1575 [W. Whittingham].

[2] *Church History*, II. 463. (This work was published during the Civil War.)

[3] For these meetings see Strype, *Eccles. Memorials*; Foxe, *Acts and Monuments*; and an undated letter from George Withers to the Elector Palatine, *Zurich Letters*, II. 160.

appointment, it was the memory of the Marian gatherings that suggested[1] the holding of similar services. As Dale[2] well says:

" When Elizabeth came to the throne the blessedness of those secret meetings for worship would not soon be forgotten. Devout men and women had learnt that in 'a small company of Christian people, united to each other by strong mutual affection and a common loyalty to Christ, it was possible to realise in a wonderful way the joy and strength of the communion of saints; and that such an assembly, though it had only a weaver or a wheelwright for its minister, might have a vivid consciousness of access to God through Christ, and might receive surprising discoveries of the divine righteousness and love."

INSISTENCE UPON UNIFORMITY PRODUCES NONCONFORMITY.

It only needed insistence upon uniformity to make explicit the implicit Nonconformity (and even, in a measure, the implicit Independency) engendered by these experiences at home and abroad. Such Nonconformity did not appear at once in Elizabeth's reign because all Protestants, even the Bishops[3], expected speedy reformation of the Church on Genevan lines. They contemplated an entire breach with Rome, not only in doctrine, but also in matters of ecclesiastical administration, government, and vestments, and it was long before they realised that the Queen had other plans.

When she made clear[4], as in her letter of Jan. 25th, 1564/5,

[1] Smith, of the Plumbers' Hall Congregation, 1567 (below, p. 7), says to the Commissioners (*A parte of a register*, 25; Grindal, *Remains*, 203):
"Then we bethought us what were best to doe, and we remembred that there was a congregation of us in this Citie in Queene Maries dayes:"
In Miles Micklebound's *Mr Henry Barrowes Platform etc.* (1611), D 2 verso, Barrowe states that in 1592, 56 persons "were taken in the very place where the persecuted Church and Martyrs were enforced to use the like exercises in Queene Maries dayes."

[2] *History of Congregationalism*, 62.

[3] See their opinions freely expressed in the *Zurich Letters*. It should be remembered that many of them had been exiles on the Continent during Mary's reign.

[4] By far the best account of the Vestiarian controversy and the rise of Nonconformity yet published is to be found in Dixon's *History of the Church of England*, Vols. v and vi.

that uniformity in rites and ceremonies must be enforced, many of the Bishops were in the unfortunate position of having to compel their brethren to conform to a "mingle-mangle" for which they themselves had no liking, and to wear vestments and perform ceremonies against the use of which they themselves had protested.

In 1566 the Royal demand for uniformity resulted in the publication of Archbishop Parker's Advertisements. Even before such publication some of the clergy had been "put out of their livings for the surplice," and at once a cleavage between Conforming and Nonconforming Puritanism appeared. How Puritanism became Separatism, and Separatism developed into Congregationalism the following pages endeavour to trace.

THE PROBLEM FOR PURITANS—TO LEAVE THE CHURCH OR REMAIN IN IT?

Immediately the more zealous of the Protestants realised that the expected reformation of the Church in a Puritan direction was not to take place, they began to ask each other: "Should we leave a Church marred by all these things which we believe to be Popish and Antichristian, or should we submit to the regulations laid upon us, remain within the Church, and do all we can there to purify it from its corruptions?"

To this question some gave one answer and some another, but there is abundant evidence to show that it is a mistake to imagine that the problem of Separation from the Church had not been thoroughly debated long before Robert Browne gathered his "companie" at Norwich[1], though it is equally plain that the earlier Separatists had not the clear and definite ideas about the nature of the Church that Browne had when he set forth his little volumes in 1582. The divergence between Conformists and Nonconformists began to appear before the Advertisements were published. In July 1565 Bishop Horne wrote to Gualter[2]:

" this matter [caps and surplices] has occasioned a great strife among us, so that our little flock has divided itself into two parties, the one

---

[1] See the present writer's *The Brownists in Norwich and Norfolk*, 1580.

[2] *Zurich Letters*, I. 142.   Cf. a most interesting letter (undated) in Grindal, *Remains*, 333 ff.

thinking that on account of this law the ministry ought to be abandoned, and the other, that it ought not."

In the following March, Parker wrote to Cecil[1]:

"I see the wilfulness of some men such, that they will offer themselves to lose all, yea, their bodies to prison, rather than they will condescend."

Men like Humphrey and Sampson, Gilby and Lever, Cartwright and Field, though they "refused the habits" and denounced the "corruptions" in the Church in very strong language, nevertheless believed it was wrong to separate from it. They were accustomed to the close connexion of Church and State, and schism was abhorrent to them; the Church's doctrinal position was their own, and they had many personal friends among its leaders; they were loth to relinquish the sanguine hopes of reformation that they had entertained, and still trusted that the influence of foreign divines would win Elizabeth over to their views; and, especially, they saw all round them masses of ignorant people, with few preachers to teach them sound doctrine, who would be left "as sheep without shepherds" and "a prey to Romish wolves," did they forsake their flocks. All these considerations helped to keep them within the Church.

Others of the clergy, however, took another view, maintaining that it was absolutely wrong to use the "remnants and relics of Popery," no matter what the circumstances might be. The decision to give up the ministry was not easily made[2], but when, on March 26th, 1566, the Archbishop demanded conformity from all the London clergy, 37 refused, including "the best, and some preachers[3]."

Some of these receded from the position they had taken up, for Grindal wrote[4] in August:

[1] *Correspondence* (Parker Soc.), 263.

[2] Cf. the letter of Coverdale, Humphrey, and Sampson to Geneva, July, 1556 [*Zurich Letters*, II. 123]. "The question, we confess, is nice and difficult, whether it is better to yield to circumstances, or to depart; to admit the relics of the Amorites, or to desert our post. Either alternative is harsh, grievous, and productive of mischief both to ourselves and the church."

[3] *Parker Corresp.* 269 f.

[4] *Zurich Letters*, I. 168–70. Cf. the long letter from Beza and Bullinger [*Zurich Letters*, II. 127–35].

" It is scarcely credible how much controversy about things of no importance has disturbed our churches, and still, in great measure, continues to do so.   Many of the more learned clergy seemed to be on the point of forsaking their ministry.   Many of the people also had it in contemplation to withdraw from us, and set up private meetings ; but however most of them, through the mercy of the Lord, have now returned to a better mind."

Others remained firm,

"so that they choose rather to lay down their functions, and leave their churches empty, than to depart one tittle from their own views[1]."

As Grindal's letter indicates, people, as well as ministers, discussed withdrawal from their parish churches.   Dr William Turner, Dean of Wells, wrote an article[2] in 1567, arguing not only against "popish ceremonies reteyned in a reformed church," but also "againste those that refuse to heare the gospell preched of such as weare the popish Englishe apparell."

THE PLUMBERS' HALL CONGREGATION.

Men who thus refused would not be satisfied without some measure of Christian fellowship and frequent assemblies for worship.   The first mention of this on record—for there seems to be no contemporary evidence for Dixon's statement[3] that Richard Fitz's congregation was arrested a month before the events now to be related—is in "The true report of our Examination and conference (as neare as wee can call to remembrance) had the 20 day of June 1567. Before the Lord Maior, the Bishop of London, the Deane of West[minster], Maister Wattes, and other Commissioners[4]."

Those examined, who have erroneously been called ministers time after time, were John Smith, William Nixon, William

---

[1] Jewel to Bullinger, Feb. 24th, 1566/7. [*Zurich Letters*, I. 185.]

[2] Peel, *Cal. of the Seconde Parte of a Register*, I. 53.

[3] *History of the Church of England*, VI. 166.

[4] This report, the running title of which is, "The Examination of certayne Londoners before the Commissioners," appears in *A parte of a register*, 23–37, and is reprinted in Grindal, *Remains*, 201–16.

White[1], James Ireland, Robert Hawkins, Thomas Boweland, Richard Morecraft, and [John Roper][2]. The two Commissioners, the Bishop of London and the Dean of Westminster, were supported by several clergymen and by the Lord Mayor. The Bishop said that they, and ten or eleven others in the Counter, were charged with absenting themselves from their parish churches, and gathering themselves together for prayer, preaching, and the administration of the Sacraments, as many as a hundred having been gathered in the Plumbers' Hall the previous day.

In reply Smith, "the ancientest of them," said that their preachers having been displaced for not subscribing, and they themselves having been summoned for not attending their parish churches,

" we bethought us what were best to doe, and we remembred that there was a congregation of us in this Citie in Queene Maries dayes: And a Congregation at *Geneva*, which used a booke and order of preaching, ministring of the Sacramentes and Discipline, most agreeable to the worde of God: which booke is alowed by that godly & well learned man, Maister *Calvin*, and the preachers there, which booke and order we nowe holde."

The discussion makes very clear throughout both the Genevan inspiration of Puritanism, and the Puritan emphasis on the Scriptures as the sole rule and guide in all ecclesiastical affairs, but only one end to it was possible. In the words of the chronicler: " From hence to prison they went all, or most part of them."

There is nothing to show that this congregation, generally called " the Plumbers' Hall congregation," was more than Separatist at this time; its members did not apparently hold any specifically Congregational view of the Church, neither had they

---

[1] See the following papers by the present writer: "William White, an Elizabethan Puritan" (*Trans. Cong. Hist. Soc.* VI. 4 ff.); "A Conscientious Objector of 1575 : A Controversy between S.B., 'An English Anabaptist' and William White, Puritan, now first printed..." (*Trans. Bapt. Hist. Soc.* VII. 71–128, and separately).

[2] Roper is mentioned in the body of the report, but not in the list of names at the head.

elected their own officers. They desired to be like "the best Reformed Churches," to have, like the Church of Scotland,

"the worde truely preached, the Sacramentes truely ministred, and Discipline according to the worde of God; & these be the notes by which the true church is known."

"PATTENSON," A SEPARATIST PREACHER.

Before the congregation is mentioned again, there is an indication in the State papers of the connexion of at least one minister with the Separatist movement.

"Master Pattenson," who had been suspended for preaching without a cure, has left on record[1] " the talk " he had with the Bishop of London in September 1567. Pattenson said that his cure was " wheresoever I do meet with a congregation that are willing to hear the word of God preached at my mouth," and when told that he must not preach without the Archbishop's licence, retorted:

"But the Archbishop of archbishops hath not suspended me from preaching, but continueth His commandments to me still: and besides that, I praise Him for it, He hath not decayed in me the gift of preaching, but rather increased it: and hath also given me a congregation that looketh that I should bestow it among them; and therefore I may not disobey Him to obey you."

Before the discussion is closed with the words, " Thus I returned to the Gatehouse, where I am now a close prisoner," it contains a reference to the Duchess of Suffolk, which is very significant in the light of other occurrences of her name[2].

BISHOP: "I sent for you because the Duchess of Suffolk hath been a suitor to me for you, that you might be at liberty. And I am contented therewith at her request, so that you will put me in two sureties that you will not preach or minister the Sacraments any more without my license or the Bishop's of Canterbury."

PATTENSON: "Her grace told me of no such sureties, neither do I mind to put in sureties to break the commandments of God. I can do that fast enough without sureties. As you do, neither mind I to make the preaching of the Gospel subject to a popish license."

[1] *State Papers Dom. Eliz.* XLIV. 20. See *Calendar*, p. 300, and Dixon, *Hist. of the Church of England*, VI. 178–80. The usual sources disclose no trace of an incumbent of the name in London at this time.

[2] See below, pp. 27–9. Dixon says that Pattenson sent this "talk" to the Duchess.

It seems clear, therefore, that in 1567 there were certainly two Separatist congregations, one that worshipped sometimes in the Plumbers' Hall, and one that welcomed the ministrations of Mr Pattenson. The two can scarcely be one and the same, for it can hardly be imagined that the "Examination of the Londoners" would have been carried through without reference to a minister, had they had one at this time. It will soon appear that there were other congregations in the city besides these two.

TRACES OF OTHER CONGREGATIONS.

Indications of this appear in lists of "active and zealous Nonconformists" given by Camden[1] and Fuller[2]. The first list contains the names of Coleman, Button, Halingham, and Benson, the second of White, Rowland (probably Bowland), and Hawkins, *i.e.* Plumbers' Hall leaders.

Of the first four named, nothing is known of Button and Halingham[3], but the names of "John Benson" and "Christofer Colman[4]" appear consecutively in the list[5] of those released from Bridewell in April 1569. About this time, too, Coleman seems to have sent a petition[6], probably to Cecil, asking for reformation of the Church according to God's Word. The petition, which is signed "Christopher Foster alias Colman," says that God will not have man's devices in His business, but obedience to His Word; the house of God has long been building, but it is far from being finished. It is good for rulers to be *in* the Church, and the chief thereof, but not *above* the Church, for that place belongs to Christ alone. The Church should be swept clean according to God's Word, and so made comparable to the best reformed churches.

[1] *Annales* (Ed. 1639), 131 (under 1568, where the name 'Puritan' is used). The first four names only are given.

[2] *Church History*, II. 547.

[3] Can this be John Holingham, one of the first Englishmen to join the English Church at Geneva? The name appears several times in Martin, *Les Protestants Anglais réfugiés à Genève.*

[4] Cooper, *Athen. Cantab.* I. 283, identifies this Coleman with an Augustinian Friar, who graduated in 1533.

[5] Below, p. 10.

[6] Strype, *Annals*, I. ii, 350–2.

THE CONGREGATION IN THE GOLDSMITH'S HOUSE, MARCH 1568.

Before examining the evidence for these congregations, it is necessary to analyse a document[1] discovered some years ago by Dr F. J. Powicke, which apparently has reference to the Plumbers' Hall flock.

On March 4th, 1567/8, 77 persons (not 72, as Mr Burrage says)—39 men and 38 women—were " fownde to gether within the parishe of St. Martens in the felde in the howse of James Tynne, gooldsmythe." The names of 72 of the 77 persons are given (the other five being wives of men mentioned), and they include six of the eight leaders of the Plumbers' Hall congregation (all but Hawkins and Roper) examined by Grindal the previous June. Other names that must be noted[2] are " Jone Evanes, Randall partridge, John Kynge, John Leonarde, and John Boulte [? Boulton]." Evidently the imprisonment imposed in June 1567 was not a long one, and on their release the prisoners had resumed their meetings, only to fall at once into the hands of the authorities, who seem to have been especially vigilant at this time. How many of the 77 taken were kept in prison is not known, nor has any report of their trial been found, but on Apl. 22nd, 1569, more than thirteen months later, 24 men and 7 women " wer dyschardged out of Brydewell." The names of the men are given[3], and they include, probably, ten of those taken in the goldsmith's house—Smith, Ireland, Nixon, Bowland, Waddy, Anderton, White, Leonard, Bolton and Lydforde (? Ludburte), and also Robert Hawkins and " John Nayshe[4]," that is to say, all the Plumbers' Hall leaders with the exception of Morecraft. A letter from Grindal to the Council[5] (Jan. 4th,

[1] *State Papers Dom. Eliz.* XLVI. 46. Printed by Dr Powicke in a useful paper on "The Early Separatists" (*Trans. Cong. Hist. Soc.* I. 141–58), and by Mr Burrage, *Early English Dissenters*, II. 9–11.

[2] See below, pp. 16, 18, 26, 33–6.

[3] British Museum, *Lansdowne MSS.* XII. ff. 67–8, from which it is given in Burrage, *Early English Dissenters*, II. 11–12.

[4] See below, pp. 36–7.

[5] *Lansdowne MSS.* XII. No. 28. Printed in Grindal, *Remains*, 316–19.

1569/70) establishes the fact that these men and women had been in prison since their arrest in March 1567/8. He says that they had been liberated in the hope that clemency would win them to obedience and good order, but their behaviour now called for severe punishment. With the letter Grindal sent a list of those whom he had released, and with it, apparently, a promise[1], made by William Bonham ["Bonam"] on May 1st, 1569, that he would not preach, or be present at any service in any place, contrary to law. Bonham, and a fellow-minister, Nicholas Crane, having preached in private houses, and administered the Sacraments there according to the Genevan book, were soon imprisoned again. In a Supplication to the Council[2], dating from this time, the members of the congregation claim that they made no promises when released, but that the Bishop gave them permission to hear the preachers they preferred rather than the clergy of their parish churches, and to have baptism according to the Genevan Order, and that "immediately after, at our request, he appointed two preachers, called Bonham and Crane, under his handwriting, to keep a lecture." Bonham having been imprisoned[3] and Crane suspended from preaching, they are now driven once again to worship in private places.

WILLIAM BONHAM AND NICHOLAS CRANE.

The few facts that are known concerning Bonham and Crane ought to be stated before leaving the story of the congregation to which they ministered. When their ministrations to this congregation first began there is no evidence to show. Their names do not occur in any of the lists that are now extant; Bonham's first appears in the promise made on May 1st, 1569, Crane's in Grindal's letter to the Council the following January.

---

[1] *Lansdowne MSS.* XII. ff. 67–8.

[2] For this supplication, see Strype, *Grindal*, 227–28.

[3] Probably this is referred to by William White, in a very outspoken letter to Grindal, dated Dec. 19th, 1569 (Peel, *Cal. Sec. Parte Reg.* I. 64–6), "And you your self allso by the authority of Gods word, ought rather to have commended and defended the zeale of such pastors and people, than at the complaint of a parasite to cast their pastor into prison without hearing his cause either before or after."

Of their life subsequent to 1570 the little that is known can be briefly stated, especially concerning Bonham. Both were included in the group of Puritan ministers that set on foot some form of Presbyterian organisation in Wandsworth in 1572[1], while Bonham was one of the ministers of similar views implicated in the Undertree conspiracy[2] in 1574. Crane was one of ten Puritan ministers who conducted an animated correspondence[3] with Thomas Cartwright in 1577, the question under discussion being whether the ministry should be forsaken when "ceremonies that are of the dregges of Poperie" are imposed. Five of these ten, including Crane, answer an undated letter from a schoolmaster[4], who had been called to a ministerial office and desired advice. He is also included in a similar group of ministers, who urged Cartwright to reply to the Rhemists' translation of the New Testament[5]. The only writing extant known to be from his pen consists of "Exceptions taken against absolute subscription to the booke of common prayer, and booke of articles[6]," an article which follows the usual Puritan lines. In fact, up to 1587, whenever Crane appears it is as a Cartwrightian Puritan who seems to have been active in working the classical system which the ministers were attempting to establish.

Sometime before that year, however, he became associated with John Greenwood, and on the 8th October they and other "Brownestes" were taken at a conventicle in Henry Martin's house, and examined in the Bishop of London's palace the same day[7].

---

[1] Bancroft, *Dangerous Positions* (Ed. 1640), 67.

[2] A sham plot, which endeavoured to associate several Puritan ministers —including Thomas Cartwright, Nicholas Standon, John Browne and Bonham—with an attempt to assassinate Archbishop Parker and the Lord Treasurer. (See *Parker Corresp.* 460–4 ; Strype, *Parker*, II. 368–72. Several letters relating to the conspiracy are in the *Lansdowne MSS.* Vol. LXIV.)

[3] Peel, *Cal. Sec. Parte Reg.* I. 136–43.

[4] *Ibid.* II. 69 f.

[5] See the preface to *A Confutation of the Rhemists' Translation.*

[6] *A parte of a register*, 119–24.

[7] See the list of those taken in Burrage, *Early Eng. Dissenters*, II. 19–24, from *State Pap. Dom. Eliz.* Vol. CCIV. (10).

He died in Newgate[1], " of the Infection of the pryson," in 1588, and Henry Barrowe[2] says that the Bishops

"would not soffer the body of this antient grave Preacher & Father M.Cr. to be carried to burial into the city through Nugate, leste the people who knew his vertue and godlines should espie and abhor their cruelty[3]."

WAS THE PLUMBERS' HALL CONGREGATION SEPARATIST?

Despite these facts, Mr Burrage argues that the Plumbers' Hall congregation was not Separatist, for he says:

(*a*) It separated not from the Church of England, but from the corruptions in the Church.

(*b*) Bonham and Crane were Puritans and not Separatists.

These reasons are surely a refinement of controversy. The congregation, it is clear, consisted of men and women who, after two imprisonments, persisted in refusing to attend their parish churches, and in gathering together in private houses. They worshipped apart from the Church of England, and used another form of service. If this is not separation in practice, what can be ? Mr Burrage is right in maintaining that there is no reason for calling the Plumbers' Hall congregation itself a Congregational Church, but there seems no adequate reason for refusing to call it Separatist.

It ought to be realised too, that in the fluid condition of religious life and ecclesiastical organisation between 1560 and 1580 it is more or less futile to attempt to fix exact and definite labels to men, churches, and even movements, to dub them Puritan, Separatist, Presbyterian, Congregational, Nonconformist, as if each of these were classes that excluded and did not overlap the others[4]. Many individuals in all classes reacted to circumstances, and advanced or receded in their views and

---

[1] Contents list of *A parte of a register*; Burrage, *Early Eng. Dissenters*, II. 46 (from *Harl. MS.* 6848, f. 55 recto).

[2] *Lansdowne MSS.* LXV. 65, printed in *Trans. Cong. Hist. Soc.* II. 269–71.

[3] Crane's widow was intimately associated with the printing of the Marprelate tracts; for a time the secret press had its abode at her house at East Molesey. (Pierce, *Hist. Intro. to the Martin Marprelate Tracts*, 152.)

[4] John Paget's *An Arrow Against the Separation of the Brownists*, though

practice in response to the needs of the state, the attitude of the authorities, the support of noblemen and gentry, or the activity or quiescence of Roman Catholics. At one time a Puritan appears to be conformist, at another nonconformist; at one moment it seems as if nothing would drive him outside of the folds of the Church, at another he speaks so strongly against its corruptions that it seems inevitable that he should separate from it. It is impossible, for example, to label William White[1] Puritan or Separatist, for at one moment he seems the one, at another time the other. The same is true of Crane. Preacher to a Separatist congregation in 1569, he nevertheless, as has been seen, continued for years after this to be a consistent supporter of the Presbyterian movement under Cartwright. Then in 1587 he is

published in 1618, and relating to the Brownists at that time, exactly describes the divergent views of Separatists half a century earlier:

" Of those that separate from the Church of God, there are many sorts: Though the Brownists assume unto themselves the title of Separation and call themselves the Churches of the Separation, yet is not this title sufficient to distinguish them; Separation being common to so many.

Of the Brownists also there are sundry sects: Some separate from the Church of England for corruptions; and yet confesse both it & Roome also to be a true Church, as the followers of Mr Johnson: Some renounce the Church of England as a false Church; and yet allow private communion with the godly therein, as Mr Robinson and his followers: Some renounce all Religious communion both publique and private with any member of that Church whosoever, as Mr Ainsworth and such as hearken unto him, being deepest and stiffest in their Schisme. The evil of this separation is great: First, the mindes of many are troubled and distracted hereby; even of such as do not separate, but have some liking thereof;...Secondly, for those that separate but do not yet joyne unto them, or being joyned do withhold from actual communion, living alone, and hearing the word of God in no Church, as some do;..."

All these classes can be more or less paralleled in the Separatist congregations between 1567–71, from simple nonconforming Puritans on the one hand to "the stiffest in their Schisme," like Richard Fitz, on the other. The things the Puritans "scrupled" were the very things that caused others to separate, while many of the Barrowists examined in 1593 declared (Burrage, *Early Eng. Diss.* II. 27–61) they had been led to their views by the preaching of Puritan ministers!

[1] See the present writer's article, "William White, An Elizabethan Puritan" (*Trans. Cong. Hist. Soc.* VI. 4 ff.), and also his *A Conscientious Objector of* 1575.

taken as a Brownist; in 1593 one of the Barrowists says he was drawn to the movement five years before, first by John Greenwood, "and since by one Crane who died in Newgate"; and in the preface to the Barrowist *True Confession of Faith* (1596) his name is the first of twenty-four of those[1] who had recently perished in London prisons. And yet Mr Burrage thinks Crane was never a real Separatist, and doubts "if ever he advanced beyond the Puritan position." What more a man can do to show he belongs to a cause than die in prison for it is not very evident; there seems to be quite as much ground for saying that Crane was a Separatist when he died as there is for saying he was a Puritan in 1572.

SEPARATISTS SENT TO SCOTLAND.

It is now necessary to return to the congregation taken in the goldsmith's house on March 4th, 1567/8, some of whom were kept in prison until April 22nd, 1569. Under the year 1568, Strype says[2] that some of those who would not conform in England had been encouraged to go to Scotland, bearing commendatory letters to the leaders of the Scottish Church. What advantage the authorities expected from this move is not plain, for on Dec. 27th, 1566, the ministers and elders of the Scottish Churches in General Assembly had sent a letter[3], drawn up by Knox, to the "Bishops and Pastors of England," protesting against the deprivation of ministers for refusing to wear the apparel, and asking that favour might be showed to them.

If the Bishops expected the Nonconformists to remain in Scotland, their hopes were soon dashed to the ground, for on May 8th, 1568—that is, less than ten weeks after the arrest—Grindal had to report to Cecil[4]:

"Our men are all returned out of Scotland; and, so far as I can learn, make no preparation to go thither again. In the meantime they

---

[1] See the list in Burrage, *Early Eng. Dissenters*, I. 153.

[2] *Grindal*, 179.

[3] *A parte of a register*, 125–7; reprinted in Neal, *History of the Puritans*, App. II. and elsewhere (the best text is in Lorimer, *John Knox and the Church of England*, 225–8).

[4] *Remains*, 295–6.

cease not here from their old practices and assemblies. It may please you to consider whether they are to be called again before you to know their meaning. One of them, named Evans[1], who is thought a man of more simplicity than the rest, hath reported (as I am credibly informed) that at Dunbar, on Good-Friday, they saw certain persons go bare-footed and bare-legged to the church, to creep to the cross. If it be so, the Church of Scotland will not be pure enough for our men. They are a wilful company. God grant them humble spirits!"

THEIR RELATIONS WITH JOHN KNOX.

It is of considerable importance to note that in Scotland the Nonconformists had dealings with John Knox. This is evident from a letter[2] written to Knox, which is interesting as an indication of the Reformer's attitude, as well as valuable for the information it contains. It is remarkable how this letter has been neglected, both before and after Lorimer drew attention to it.

Knox's concern with the unrest in the English Church and his general sympathy with the Puritans is shown by the letter from the General Assembly of the Scottish Church to the Bishops at the end of 1566[3]. That there was a limit to this sympathy first finds expression in a letter[4], dated Feb. 14th, 1567/8, to John Wood, Secretary to the Regent Murray, then living in England, in which he says:

"The truth of God hath now, of some years, been manifested to both [England and Scotland]; but what obedience the words, works, and behaviour of men give sufficient testimony. The defence and maintenance of superstitious trifles produced never better fruit, in the end, than I perceive is budding amongst you—*schism*—which, no doubt, is a forerunner of greater desolation, unless there be speedy repentance. God comfort that dispersed little flock (*i.e.*, the English Congregation at Geneva) amongst whom I once lived with quietness of conscience and contentment of heart, and amongst whom I would be content to end my days, if so it might stand with God's good pleasure...."

Not knowing of this letter, but no doubt encouraged to write

---

[1] "Jone Evanes in Holborne" was one of the goldsmith's congregation. He does not appear as one of those liberated in 1569, so perhaps he was not sent to prison again. But see below, pp. 18, 26.

[2] In *The Seconde Parte of a Register*. Printed by Lorimer, 298–300.

[3] Above, p. 15.   [4] Lorimer, 240.

by the Assembly's letter of 1566, some of the imprisoned Separatists wrote to Knox. His reply is not extant, but its nature can be gathered from the letter Lorimer prints[1], the date of which is determined as May 1568 by a reference to Mary's escape from Lochleven[2]. The unknown writer says:

"Dearly beloved, in the first letter that ye wrote in answer to our letter when we were in the Fleete, it seemeth that ye are not well contented that we did not communicate with other Churches. That is known both to God and men, and other good Churches, and by four years—what troubles a great many godly suffered in that space, how we were handled by the Popish court both in Popish excommunication and imprisonment, for that we would not go back again to the wafer-cake and kneeling, and to other knackles of Popery. That persecution grew so fast as that it brought many a hundred to know one another that never knew before; and we joined all with one heart and mind to serve God with pure hearts and minds according to his Word. And where ye say, The matter is weighty for it condemneth the public ministry of England, let them take heed of that with your Church in Scotland, and the French and Dutch Church in England. We desire no other order than you hold; and to come back from an Apostolical Church, by Gods grace we mind not, but rather to take imprisonment, exilement, or what other crosses the Lord shall lay upon us. And if God justify our doings, if all men in the world were against us, it is no matter. And if the Lord condemn us, and all men should justify our doings, we were in a miserable case."

Apparently, after receiving Knox's first letter here mentioned, the writer of the present letter visited Scotland, probably as one of those referred to by Grindal[3]. To him Knox evidently gave a sealed letter for his imprisoned brethren, concerning which he now writes:

"Our brethren do give harty thanks for your gentle letter written unto them; but, to be plain with you, it is not in all points liked; and for my part, if I had known the tenor of it, when I was with you, I would have said many words that I never spake. We all agree well with your judgment that they shall not escape the judgments of God, without harty repentance, for molesting and troubling the hearts and consciences of the godly, and for mainteyning things

---

[1] Lorimer, *op. cit.* 298–300.

[2] "It is no small grief to my heart to hear the news that is with you, how that the Queen is broken forth out of prison, and hath 4000 men with her."

[3] Above, pp. 15, 16.

in the Church for which, by the word of God, they have no ground. But when you say you cannot allow those that obstinately do refuse to hear the message of salvation at such mens mouths as please not us in all things, so say we. I know no man in our Congregation that doth obstinately refuse the Word of life. But when you say at such mens mouths, no doubt there be many men that be authorized to preach that are both hereticks and wicked Papists, which the Church of England doth allow; and if you mean them, then we say we utterly refuse to hear them, and also all those that do maintain this mingle-mangle ministry, Popish order and Popish apparel which is to the great grief of the godly, and can take no comfort of such doctrine....

Whereas you wish that our consciences had a better ground, truly we cannot see by these Scriptures that should alter our consciences from a Reformed Church that hath those marks, to go back to mixtures. Although it be but a poor Church and under perils and persecutions, and have many enemies both open and familiar friends against it, and have no authority to defend it, and since our departure from you more enemies we have a great many, which seem somewhat to take hold of you for the defence of them, that they may the more cruelly handle us, as some of our brethren feeleth it, and is grown by the party that went away from us, which now is in great favour of the Bishop, which never was before, and hath told him and all others that you are flat against us and condemn all our doings. But this is our comfort, the Lord Jesus is with us. At his coming home he did openly stand against the whole Church with many reviling words, and no gentle nor honest means could persuade him, whereupon the Church hath excommunicated him."

That is to say, one of the Nonconformists who had been in Scotland forsook his brethren on his return, advertised the fact that Knox did not favour the attitude of the Separatists, and, withstanding the Church to which he belonged, was excommunicated by it. It will soon be possible[1] to identify this excommunicated person with some measure of certainty.

The tenor of this letter—especially the reference to "our Congregation" and the fact that the congregation so far exercised discipline as to excommunicate one of its members—indicates the existence of a real Separatist Church. Nevertheless, even this church was not deliberately and definitely Congregational. Its members say that they desire no order but that of the Scottish Church, and they were only compelled to become "Congregational" by circumstances.

[1] See below, p. 26.

The doubtful point here is whether the letter refers to the goldsmith's house congregation as a whole, as the mention of Evans suggests, or to some other congregation, possibly comprising many who met at the goldsmith's house and in the Plumbers' Hall, who were prepared to go farther on the road to Separation than the whole congregation was willing to travel.

THOMAS LEVER AND SEPARATIST PRISONERS.

Before considering some facts that help to answer this question, it should be noted that Thomas Lever[1], a very outspoken opponent of the ceremonies, took the same attitude as Knox. The collection of documents[2] which contains the Separatist's letter to Knox, contains also "the copie of a writing delivered to the prisoners of Brydewell the 5 of December 1568 by Mr. Tho. Lever, precher." Lever had conferred with these prisoners, and, in response to their requests, states his own views. He purposed "to avoyde the square capp, the surplice, the kneeling at the Communion, and such like garments and rit[e]s," and utterly condemns the urging and observing of them more than God's commandments. But he does not condemn those who differ from him and use the ceremonies, and as the Church of England has the Gospel preached and the Sacraments administered truly "in matters of substance," he believes it is wrong to leave it because of the ceremonies.

These prisoners were in *Bridewell*, the prison from which 24 men and 7 women were released the following April. Are they the same as "the brethren" to whom the letter written to Knox refers? The writer of that letter speaks of "the first letter that ye wrote in answer to our letter when we were in the *Fleete*," but he does not say where the congregation was when the second letter was written. It is therefore not possible to determine whether the two congregations were, or were not, the same.

---

[1] See the *Dictionary of National Biography*.
[2] Peel, *Cal. Sec. Parte Reg.* I. 54–5.

EVIDENCE INDICATING EXISTENCE OF SEVERAL CONGREGATIONS.

If the development has been made plain, it should now be clear that at this time there were several congregations meeting in London. Confirmation of this appears in the oft-quoted passages in the *Calendar* of Spanish Letters and State Papers. On the 16th Feb. 1567/8, the Ambassador reports[1]:

" About a week ago they discovered here a newly invented sect, called by those who belong to it 'the pure or stainless religion.' They met to the number of 150 in a house where their preacher used a half tub for a pulpit, and was girded with a white cloth. Each one brought with him whatever food he had at home to eat, and the leaders divided money amongst those who were poorer, saying that they imitated the life of the apostles and refused to enter the temples to partake of the Lord's supper as it was a papistical ceremony. This having come to the ears of the city authorities, they, in accord with the Queen's Council, sent 40 halberdiers to arrest the people. They found them meeting in the house, and arrested the preacher and five of the principals, leaving the others, and have appointed persons to convert them."

Although the reports betray an ignorance and a degree of exaggeration not difficult to understand in a foreigner, they are extremely suggestive. On Feb. 28th, the account is continued[2]. After summarising the events related in the letter of Feb. 16th, the record says:

" Another of their meeting places has been found, and six of the principal members of this congregation, too, have been arrested. I am told by a well-informed Catholic that he is certain there are 5000 of them in this city alone."

Again, on March 14th, he writes[3]:

"Orders have been given to release the people who call themselves members of the pure or apostolic religion, on condition that within 20 days they conform to the religion of the State or leave the country."

Finally, on June 26th, the account states[4]:

" In spite of the threats made to the sect called the Puritans, to prevent their meeting together, I am informed that recently as many as 400 of them met near here, and, although a list of their

---

[1] *Calendar*, Vol. II. *Eliz.* 1568–79, 7.
[2] *Ibid.* 11.   [3] *Ibid.* 12.   [4] *Ibid.* 43.

names was taken, only six of them were arrested, in order to avoid scandal and also because they have their influential abettors."

With these reports, the following significant extract from John Stowe's *Memoranda*[1], dated 1567/8, should be carefully compared:

"About that time were many congregations of the Anabaptists in London, who called themselves Puritans or Unspotted Lambs of the Lord. They kept their church in the Minories with out *Algate*. Afterwards they assembled in a ship or lighter in *St Katheryns Poole*, then in a chopper's house, nigh *Wolle Key* in Thames St., where only the goodman of the house and the preacher, whose name was Brown, (and his auditory were called the Brownings), were committed to ward; then afterward in *Pudynge Lane* in a minister's house in a blind alley, and seven of them were committed to the Counter in the Poultry. Then after, on the 29th of February, being Shrove Sunday, at *Mountjoye Place*, where the bishop, being warned by the constables, bade let them alone. Then at *Westminster*, the 4 of March, and in a goldsmith's house near to the *Savoy*, the 5 of March, where being taken to the number of 60 and odd, only three were sent to the Gatehouse. In many other places were and are the like. On Easter day at *Hogston* in my Lord of London's man's house to the number of 120, and on Low Sunday in a carpenter's house in *Aldermanbury*. It is to be noted that such as were at any time committed for such congregating were soon delivered without punishment."

Leaving on one side for the moment[2] the preacher "Brown," and merely mentioning the discrepancy of one day in the reference to the congregation in the goldsmith's house, it should be noticed that these extracts suggest that not only were there several congregations in the city at this time, but that the same congregation had several meeting places. This is borne out by the letter[3] sent by Grindal to Bullinger on June 11th, 1568:

[1] *Three Fifteenth-Century Chronicles with Historical Memoranda by John Stowe* [Camden Soc.], 143. The spelling has been modernised, with the exception of the italicised place names.

[2] Below, pp. 27–30.

[3] *Zurich Letters*, I. 201–5. Cf. an important letter from Bishop Cox to Gualter (*ibid.* I. 234–8) nearly three years afterwards, in which, he says that neither the authority of state, queen, or church, nor the warnings of divines at home and abroad, affect the disturbers of the Church's peace, "who by the vehemence of their harangues have so maddened the wretched multitude, and driven some of them to that pitch of frenzy, that they now obstinately refuse to enter our churches, either to baptise their children,

"Our controversy concerning the habits, about which you write, had cooled down for a time, but broke out again last winter; and this by the means of some who are more zealous than they are either learned or gifted with pious discretion. Some London citizens of the lowest order, together with four or five ministers, remarkable neither for their judgment nor learning, have openly separated from us; and sometimes in private houses, sometimes in the fields, and occasionally even in ships, they have held their meetings and administered the sacraments. Besides this, they have ordained ministers, elders, and deacons, after their own way, and have even excommunicated some who had seceded from their church. And because masters Laurence Humphrey, Sampson, Lever, and others, who have suffered so much to obtain liberty in respect of things indifferent, will not unite with them, they now regard them as semi-papists, and will not allow their followers to attend their preaching. The number of this sect is about two hundred, but consisting of more women than men. The privy council have lately committed the heads of this faction to prison, and are using every means to put a timely stop to this sect."

These facts fit in exactly with other contemporary evidence that has so far been quoted, though it is possible that the Bishop's "two hundred" is an underestimate, and certain that the Spanish Ambassador's "5000" is altogether too large.

A CONGREGATION WITH A COVENANT.

The quotations made in the foregoing pages concerning the developments in the year 1568 are more or less familiar to all students of the subject. It is now possible to add to them some new facts that will enable the various congregations to be identified with some degree of assurance, for valuable evidence is afforded by two undated treatises[1] written by a member of a Separatist congregation about this time, and by the reply to them[2].

The first treatise gives fifteen causes from God's Word why it is wrong to worship and communicate "with those that do

or to partake of the Lord's supper, or to hear sermons. They are entirely separated both from us and from those good brethren of ours [*i.e.* the Puritan ministers]; they seek bye paths; they establish a private religion, and assemble in private houses, and there perform their sacred rites, as the Donatists of old, and the Anabaptists now."

[1] Peel, *Cal. Sec. Parte Reg.* Nos. 32 and 33 (I. 55–59).
[2] *Ibid.* I. 59–61

either receive or mainteine the remnants, reliques and levings of the pope and papistry." Emphatic protest is made against the imposition of uniformity in ceremonies, the licensing of preachers, and their deprivation for non-subscription. Most important, however, is the 15th reason, which shows that the writer belonged to a Separatist Church, the members of which had made a definite covenant with each other. It reads:

" I have now joyned my self to the Church of Christ wherin I have yielded my selfe subject to the discipline of Gods Word as I promised at my Baptisme, which if I should now again forsake and joyne my self with the traditioners, I should then forsake the union wherein I am knyt with the body of Christ, and joyne myselfe to the discipline of Antichrist. For in the church of the traditioners there is none other Discipline, but that which hath bene ordeined by the Antichristian popes of Rome, wherby the Church of God hath allwaies benn afflicted, and is to this day, for which I refuse them."

This declaration[1] is exactly repeated in the second treatise, which is subscribed " Fare ye well, my deere brethren, all you that beleve in Jesus Christ," and is described in the MS. Contents List as " The private churches against popish ceremonies."

The writer of the second treatise is " a simple, unlearned, man," who is determined not to " come back againe to the preachings of them that have receaved the marke of the Romish beast." He speaks with great boldness of limits to the Royal power:

" Neverthelesse, this is out of doute, that the Quenes highnes hath not authoritie to compell anie man to beleeve any thing contrary to Gods word, nether may the subject geve her grace the obedience, in case he do his soule is lost for ever without repentaunce. Our bodyes, goodes, and lives be at her commaundement, and she shall have them as of true subjects. But the soule of man for religion is bound to none but unto God and his holy word."

Neither does he mince matters when speaking of the ceremonies:

" Antichrist, the Pope of Rome, this name is banished out of England, but his body, which be the bishops and other shavelings do not only remayne, but also his tayle, which be his filthy traditions, wicked lawes, and beggerly ceremonies,...yea, and the whole body of his pestiferous canon lawe."

---

[1] As will be seen below (pp. 37–38), it reappears in one of the papers relating to Richard Fitz's congregation, in a document endorsed by Archbishop Parker and placed by Strype in the year 1573, and as late as 1581.

His most violent words, however, are kept for those to whom he writes, men who "dissemble one way or other to save their pigges, yea though they do put their names in the Popes bookes."

To them he says:

"Seeing it hath pleased God to geve all true Christians a priviledge to seeke a true reformation in religion, and to flee and avoyde all polutions of antichrist, choosing of ministers elders, and deacons, whosoever goeth about to hinder and slaunder this good cause, the dogges shall eate his fleshe and licke his blood without the honour of a sepulchre. Take heed, therefore, you calking cavillers, you moun-grels, slidebacks, hyrelings and tymeservers, with your tryfling toyes which be but apishe, least you drinke of the cuppe of Gods wrathe with the Papists....And, deerely beloved in the Lord, you go to your parish churche, and ther stand up and say, I beleve in God, yet you do but mocke with God so long as you walke in those wicked lawes of Antichriste and mainteyne his knightes the bishops with such inordinat riches and unlawfull autoritie, so long shall you never banishe the monstruous beast, the Pope, out of England."

THE COMMUNITY FROM WHICH THIS CONGREGATION SECEDED—MINISTER, JOHN BROWNE.

Additional information concerning these treatises is furnished by a letter[1], which is clearly a reply to the second of them[2], if not to both. It is written by "John Browne, Minister," and subscribed, "Written the 18th of March, Yours in the Lord to the death," but unfortunately the year is not given.

This letter makes plain that Browne belongs to a Separatist church, in which the writer of the second treatise (probably of both treatises) once held office[3], but from which he and his friends have seceded, and

"refuse your place and standinge in this buildinge, and stande still as lookers on, and do nothing therin except to the plucking downe of the same; as you do by separating, when as you will not joyne with us according to his worde."

[1] Peel, *Cal. Sec. Parte Reg.* I. 59–61.

[2] Witness, for example, the reference to "the doggs shall lick his bloud" in the quotations immediately above in the text, and in the reply below, p. 25.

[3] Browne says: "I call your building private in comparison of that it was *when you occupied your office in this Church* together with the rest of your brethren" (italics the present writer's).

Possibly Browne and his flock were in the habit[1] of attending parish churches where there were "forward preachers," and this was one of the causes of the secession. He tells the seceders that the "private assembling of yourselves together...hindereth Gods glorie," and in dividing themselves "from a christian Congregation gathered together according to His word" they separate themselves "from salvation."

Then follow these very informing sentences[2]:

" Now I would in God that seeing not onely that you have professed the Gospell, but allso have borne some burthen with your brethren, and have suffred both heat and sweat, yea, and in plucking up the weedes, the thornes have pricked you very sharply. But if you should now refuse to plucke up the weedes for fear of pricking with the thornes, you should then shew yourselves to have begun in the spirite and end in the flesh, which God forbid.

Alas, with what hart can you alow that sentence among others which compareth *the small congregation that is gathered together in this city* to Naboths vineyard, which whosoever doth dissolve or breake up, the doggs shall lick his bloud, without the honour of a sepulchre, with what face or hart, I say, can you allow this sentence? *Seeing you are no small occasions yourself of the dissolving or breaking up of this litle vineyeard or Church of God, for through your ensample the weake are driven backe, the reste are kept in a stay, the godly are grieved, and the enemies rejoice and say that you have a Church alone by your selves, and Fitz hath another by himself etc. So that thei account 4 or 5 Churches divided one from another, so that one of them either cannot or will not joyne one with another.* But woe be unto them (saith our Saviour Christ) by whome offence come etc.

For where was it ever seene in time of persecution, when a companie were gathered together out of divers places into one felowshipp, and had suffred for the truth together, that it should be lawfull for them to be divided into divers and sundry felowshippes or Congregations, so that either they will not or can not come together."

The seceders are then blamed because they meet secretly and not openly, and they are told that

"whosoever either doth excommunicate himself, or is excommunicated by other...is counted no member of Christ."

[1] Cf. the discussions between Robert Browne and Robert Harrison on this point (Peel, *The Brownists in Norwich and Norfolk*, 1580), the letter from Geneva (below, p. 42), and Grindal's letter (above, p. 22).

[2] Italics the present writer's.

To this statement there is the useful marginal note:

> "And what you have judged of [him] that, being excommunicate, will not reconcile himselfe againe, might appeare in the wordes you spake to me for keepinge of company with Evans."

It has been seen[1] that one who returned from Scotland in 1568 was excommunicated by the church to which he belonged. The only name left on record of those who were sent to Scotland is that of the simple Evans, who found favour with the Bishop of London. From this note it is evident that Evans was an excommunicated person, and therefore it seems extremely likely that John Evans was the member of the Church who was excommunicated on his return from the north.

CONGREGATIONS SO FAR DISCLOSED.

Before stating evidence that helps to clear up certain doubtful points, it may be well to summarise the congregations so far disclosed.

1. *The Plumbers' Hall congregation.* Its demands were Puritan, and it desired to follow the Genevan and Scottish Churches. It separated from the Church of England because of many "corruptions" therein. The *congregation in the goldsmith's house* seems to have been composed largely of the same individuals as the one that met in the Plumbers' Hall.

2. There were many other congregations, probably believing in different degrees of Separation. Some of these may have been formed by members of (1), who wanted to go further; others may have been formed independently, and then, perhaps, joined by seceders from (1).

3. By one of these congregations, or perhaps by the goldsmith's, Evans was excommunicated on his return from Scotland. The church that excommunicated him, while emphatically Separatist, yet "desired no other order" than that of the Church of Scotland.

4. John Browne was minister to a congregation, from which

---

[1] Above, pp. 16, 18.

many had seceded to join other churches, of one of which Richard Fitz was minister.

Connected with one or other of these congregations as ministers are William Bonham, Nicholas Crane, and Mr Pattenson.

JOHN BROWNE (AND "THE BROWNINGS")
—SOMETIMES CONFUSED WITH ROBERT BROWNE.

Stowe says that the preacher of one of the Separatist congregations " was Brown (and his auditory were called the Brownings)." It is now clear that his name was John Browne. Can he be identified ? Presumably so, and in view of Mr Burrage's suggestion[1] that Stowe confused the Brownings with Robert Browne's followers, it is important to note that confusion between the two Brownes has occurred in more recent years. Students have often been puzzled by Dexter's statement[2], following Strype[3], that Robert Browne was chaplain to the Roman Catholic Duke of Norfolk in 1571/2. The letter quoted in this connexion was sent by Archbishop Parker and other Ecclesiastical Commissioners to the Duchess of Suffolk on Jan. 13th, 1571/2, demanding that " one Brown, your Grace's chaplain," should be sent " to answer such matter as he is to be charged withal." The letter is printed in the *Parker Correspondence*[4], where it is rightly addressed to the Duchess of Suffolk, with a note stating that Strype was wrong in saying that it was sent to the Duke of Norfolk.

He was equally wrong in his conjecture that " one Brown " was Robert Browne, for the mention of the Duchess of Suffolk enables him to be identified as John Browne, minister to a Separatist congregation whose " auditory were called the Brownings."

[1] *Early English Dissenters*, I. 84 n. The suggestion may or may not be right. It is surely as possible that John Browne's followers were called *Brownings*, as that Robert's were labelled *Brownists*, and the one name died while the other lived. See on ' The name Brownist,' below, p. 48.

[2] *Congregationalism as seen in its Literature*, 64.

[3] *Parker*, II. 68, where the date is also given incorrectly as *June* 13. Dexter follows Strype's here also.

[4] P. 390, from the MS. in the Inner Temple Library, No. 538, Vol. 47, f. 507.

THE DUCHESS OF SUFFOLK.

When the Ecclesiastical Commissioners wrote to the Duchess, they said that they understood she had refused to let her chaplain come before the Commissioners, claiming " a priviledged place for his defence," and they informed her that their jurisdiction extended " to all places, as well exempt, as not exempt, within her Majesty's dominions, and before this time never by any called into question." In thus defending extreme Protestants, Katherine Brandon, Dowager Duchess, was but acting in accordance with her previous history[1]. Widowed in 1545, she had married Richard Bertie in 1552, and her outspoken Protestantism had so offended Stephen Gardiner that it was unsafe for her to stay in the country when Mary became Queen. Early in 1555, in disguise, and with much difficulty and risk, she escaped, and, after many adventures, she and her husband found their way to Wesel. Cold and hungry, they were about to pass the night in a church porch (though shelter and care were imperative, as the Duchess was near to child-birth), when they fell in with Francis de Rivers, minister of the refugee Walloon Church in the town. He at once returned the kindness the Duchess had shown to him and other religious exiles in England during Edward's reign by securing them a comfortable cottage, where Peregrine Bertie, Lord Willoughby de Eresby, was born on Oct. 12th. Bertie found that he and his wife were still within range of persecution at Wesel, and they moved on to Strassburg, and afterwards to Weinheim, from whence they received an invitation from the King of Poland, who had been informed by John A'Lasco of their distress[2].

[1] See the lives of Katherine, her husband, and her son in the *Dictionary of National Biography*.

[2] *Brieff discours off the troubles begonne at Franckford*, 184 f., where, after describing the departure of the Duchess from Wesel, the writer says: " The congregation that was at Wezell wantinge amonge them, partly the comforte whiche many of them had, by M[r] B[ertie] and my L[ady] beinge there, and partly also other reasonable considerations movinge them; they left Wesel and folowed after: But passinge by Franckf. and perceavinge the contention to be amonge them so boilinge hott, that it ran over on both sides, and yet no fier quenched: many had small pleasure to stay there, but went to Basil and other places, ..."

THE CONNEXION OF THE DUCHESS AND OF JOHN BROWNE WITH THE ENGLISH CHURCH AT FRANKFORT.

John Browne's acquaintance with the Duchess of Suffolk no doubt began during the time of exile, if it had not done so previously. Bertie was asked[1] by the magistrate at Frankfort to be one of three arbiters in the disputes among the English congregation there, and Browne's name occurs several times in the volume in which those disputes are described.

On Sept. 29th, 1557, he and ten other Englishmen had written[2] [no place given, but clearly from Strassburg] to Frankfort, offering a form of reconciliation, which Ashley and his supporters did not accept. Among the eleven were Francis and Henry Knollys, and Francis Wilford, and these, with John Browne, are given[3] as joining the Frankfort Church in December 1557. Browne was one of those who subscribed[4] the "new discipline," and he was still at Frankfort in January 1559, when he is a signatory of a letter to the English Church at Geneva[5].

The Duchess returned soon after Elizabeth's accession, but the date of Browne's home-coming is not known.

BROWNE ASSOCIATED WITH BOTH PURITANS AND SEPARATISTS.

John Browne is a common name[6], and it would have been dangerous to identify the exile with John Browne of the Brownings ten years later, did not a connecting link exist in the fact that Mr Pattenson, another minister of a nonconforming congregation, was also a protégé of the Duchess of Suffolk[7]. Browne's name also appears with that of Bonham as one of those impli-

---

[1] *Brieff discours off the troubles begonne at Franckford*, 99.
[2] *Ibid.* 170–4.   [3] *Ibid.* 134.
[4] *Ibid.* 134.   [5] *Ibid.* 188–90.
[6] Several "John Brownes" appear in Newcourt's *Repertorium*, but there is no incumbent of the name in 1568, except the Vicar of "Walden," and he died in 1570.
[7] Above, pp. 8, 9.

cated in the Undertree conspiracy[1], and he seems to have acted frequently with the "more forward" of the Puritan ministers.

For example, he visited Field and Wilcox when they were in prison in 1573, and he is included[2] with the two just named and Dering, Wyborn, and Johnson (all Puritan ministers), and with Sparrow and King, members of Richard Fitz's Separatist congregation, in a group examined by the Council "about Cartwright's book[3]" and other matters. Five articles were put to them, and it is said that Browne, Wyborn, Dering, and Johnson answered in the negative to the first article, viz. "Whether it be lawful for a private man openly to disprove or condemn in doctrine, that thing that is established by public authority, before he hath by humble supplication shewed the error thereof to the said authority; expressing his name and hand to the same?"

In Strype's words:

"The issue of the appearance and examination of these men was this. The Council took order, that Dering should not read his lectures at St Paul's; nor the other three, Wyborn, Johnson, and Brown, preach till further order. It was then said to Field and Wilcox, that they should return again to their lodging, but the day following to Newgate. Whereof they, the Council, could not dispense, being so set down by statute, except the Queen would pardon them. Which if they could not obtain, they should be banished the realm for disliking our book of religion. And after, it was said to Sparrow and King, that they should return to their prisons; and if they would not agree to our religion, they should be banished also. How they got off I know not, but I think they suffered no infliction of banishment as was threatened them."

The value of this examination lies in the fact that Puritan ministers and known Separatist laymen appear together, John Browne, who evidently worked with both, appearing with them. Browne must have been living in 1574, when his name appears in connexion with the Undertree plot, but nothing is known of his life after 1573 or of the date and circumstances of his death[4].

---

[1] Above, p. 12 and *Lansdowne MSS.*, LXIV.

[2] Strype, *Parker*, II. 238–41. Browne is called the Chaplain to the Duchess of Suffolk on this account, which Strype obtained from a manuscript in the Inner Temple Library, No. 538, Vol. 47, f. 479.

[3] No doubt *A Replye to an answere*, which was published early in 1573.

[4] An interesting item in the present writer's *Cal. Sec. Parte Register*, I. 61–2 (immediately following Browne's reply to the Separatist treatises)

RICHARD FITZ'S CONGREGATION.

The mention of Sparrow and King as members of Richard
Fitz's congregation made it necessary that the references to
that congregation should be examined in detail at this point.
Mr Burrage, in his attempted re-construction[1] of the history of
Puritanism and Separatism at this period, declares that Grindal
referred to the Plumbers' Hall congregation in his letter of
June 11th, 1568, when he said[2] four or five ministers "have
openly separated...they have ordained ministers, elders, and
deacons, after their own way, and have even excommunicated
some who had seceded from their church." Mr Burrage further
holds that the seceders from the Plumbers' Hall congregation
here mentioned joined Richard Fitz's congregation.

This reading of events may be the correct one, but the
solution of the problem is probably not quite so simple[3], for
there is nothing to prove that Grindal had the Plumbers' Hall
congregation distinctly in his mind; there are no signs of the

should not be overlooked. It consists of (1) A Letter to "Mr Browne,
Minister of the Word of God"; and (2) "Ten Questions put forth by
Mr Browne...after the Receat of this Letter, and the same answered as
followeth." This is described in a Contents Lists as "Mr Brownes Questions
and Mr Sheringtons Answears." Of Sherington nothing is known, but his
letter and answer exhibit a belief in tolerance quite uncommon at this time.
He asks the Bishops, who believe in the ceremonies, and Browne "and the
rest," who are opposed to them, to remember Christian liberty, which gives
a man the right "to use or refuse" these things.

"The one side binding men to receive them. The other binding men
to refuse them, and thus taketh the liberty which Christians ought to have
in them quite away, and of this followeth, the one side will not suffer those
ministers which preach Jesus Christ truly unless they take them. Again
the other will not hear them and will rather be forbidden and cease to preach
Christ Jesus at all then to weare them."

Browne asks:

"Whether he denieth the Liberty of Christians that saith no Christian
man should have to do with anything of Antichrist, yea or no?"

The reply is:

"He denieth the liberty of a Christian which doth not with St. Paul
becom like to all men to winn all men to Christ...."

[1] *Early English Dissenters*, I. 79–93.   [2] Above, p. 22.

[3] Witness the number of congregations in the summary above, p. 26

association of "four or five ministers" with that congregation in 1568; and it must not be overlooked that a contemporary writer states[1] that four or five other congregations existed, one of which was Fitz's.

THREE PAPERS RELATING THERETO.

Recent investigators have had before them three papers relating to Fitz's congregation, papers which Mr Burrage has printed in full[2]. These must be summarised before further evidence can be considered:

1. *The first*[3], headed "The trewe markes of Christes churche" states "The order of the privye churche[4] in London whiche by the malice of Satan is falselie slaundred, and evell spoken of," and is signed "Richarde Fytz, Minister." The "trewe markes" are said to be:

"Fyrste and formoste, the Glorious worde and Evangell preached, not in bondage and subjection, but freely, and purelye. Secondly to have the Sacraments mynistred purely, onely and all together accordinge to the institution and good worde of the Lorde Jesus, without any tradicion or invention of man. And laste of all, to have, not the fylthye Cannon lawe, but dissiplyne onelye, and all together agreable to the same heavenlye and almighty worde of oure good Lorde, Jesus Chryste."

That, it will be observed, is a typical Puritan statement, with nothing specifically congregational about it.

2. *The second paper*, also in black letter[5], is considered below[6].

3. *The third*[7], a manuscript, endorsed "B. of London. Puretans," is dated by internal evidence as the 13th year of Elizabeth's reign, and is signed by 11 men and 16 women.

---

[1] Above, p. 25.   [2] *Early English Dissenters*, II. 13–18.

[3] In black letter. *State Pap. Dom. Eliz., Add.* xx. 107 (1).

[4] Note "*The* privy church." Was there only one at this time, or did Fitz hold that his was "*the* privy church," and the others had no claim to the title? Compare the title of the second treatise examined above (pp. 23, 24). "The private *churches* against popish ceremonies."

[5] *State Pap. Dom. Eliz.* xx. 107 (11).   [6] pp. 37 ff.

[7] *Ibid.* xx. 107.

It is both a petition for purity in worship and a defence of separation, and it gives extremely valuable information concerning the organization and personnel of the church. Part of it reads:

"Therefore according to the saying of the almighty our god—[Matt. xviii. 20] wher ij or iij are gathered in my name ther am I. So we a poore congregation whom god hath seperated from the churches of englande and from the mingled and faulse worshipping therin used, out of the which assemblies the lord our onely Saviour hath called us, and still calleth, saying cume out from among them, and seperate your selves from them & touche no unclean thing, then will I receyve you, and I wilbe your god and you shalbe my sonnes and doughters sayth the lord. [2 Cor. vi. 17–18.] so as god geveth strength at this day we do serve the lord every saboth day in houses, and on the fourth day in the weke we meet or cum together weekely to use prayer & exercyse diciplyne on them whiche do deserve it, by the strength and sure warrant of the lordes good word as in [Mt. xviii. 15–18, 1 Cor. v.], but wo be unto this cursed cannon Lawe the gayne[?] wherof hath caused the byshopes and clargi of england to forsake the right way and have gone astray, followyng the way of baalam sonn of bosor [2 Pet. ii. 15], which have throughe their pompe and couvetousnesse broughte the gospell of our saviour Jesus christ into suche sclaunder and contempte, that men do thinke for the most part that the papistes do use and hold a better religion then those which call them selves christians, and ar not, but do lye [Rev. iii. 9] the holy gost sayth. I behold another beast cummyng up out of the earthe which had ij hornes lyke the lame, so this secrete and disguysed antechrist to wit, this cannon law with [?] the braunshes and [?] their [?] maintayners thoughe not so openly, have by lon[g]e imprisonment pyned & kylled [Matt. xxiii. 34–35] the lordes servants (as our minister Rycherd fitz) thomas bowlande deacon | one partryge | & gyles fouler | and besydes them a great multitude, which no man could number of all nations and people and tounges [Rev. vii. 9] whose good cause and faythfull testimony though we should cease to grone and crye unto our god to redresse such wronges & cruell handelynges of his pore memberes, the very walles of the prisons about this citye, as the gatehouse, brydewell, the counters, the kynges benche, the marcialsey, the whyte lyon, would testifye godes anger kyndlyde agynst this land for suche injustyce and subtyll persecucion."

ANALYSIS OF THE NAMES OF MEMBERS
OF THE CONGREGATION.

Of the thirty-one names in the body and at the foot of this document, several are familiar. Thomas Bowlande, deacon, was one of the leaders of Plumbers' Hall congregation examined by Grindal &c. on June 20th, 1567, and he, Randall Partridge, Edye Burre [Burris], John King, John Leonarde, Eliz. Balfurth [Bamford], Eliz. Slacke, and possibly Elizabeth Leonardes [?John's wife] were among those taken in the goldsmith's house[1].

Of Fitz absolutely nothing is known, neither is it certain when his congregation first met. This petition makes quite clear, however, that it was deliberately and emphatically Separatist, and that it had both elected officers and exercised discipline over its members. Of its elder, John Bolton, nothing is said, no doubt because the congregation felt that he was a cause of shame rather than glory. Bolton has been an exile during Mary's reign, joining the English church at Geneva on Nov. 5th, 1556[2]. He next appears as a member of the congregation taken in the goldsmith's house in March 1568, and as released from prison in April 1569. He joined Fitz's congregation, and became an elder, but afterwards made a recantation at Paul's Cross. For this he was excommunicated by the church, and afterwards (before 1576) committed suicide[3].

---

[1] Probably there were others, for the surnames King, Ireland, Sparrow and Stokes [Stockes] appear in both lists; Annes Hall may be Annys Hawkes, and Annes Evanes a relative of John.

[2] Martin, *Les Protestants Anglais réfugiés à Genève* 1555–1560, 333.

[3] References to Bolton's history and fate are so persistent that they deserve more than a bare summary. Ainsworth, in his *Counterpoyson* 39, answering the charge that God had testified against Separation because Bolton had hanged himself, says:

"Bolton (one of the Elders of that separated church wherof Mr Fits was Pastour in the beginning of Queen Elizabeths reigne,) first revolted at Pauls Crosse, was reproved and excommunicated for this by the church, and after, not having grace to return or repent, hanged himself. This is testified to me by one yet living among us, who was then a member of that church, and wel acquainted with the affairs thereof, and with this matter, and saw the man dead. Which being so, Boltons martyrdom is little for the credit of your cause and church, wherof he died a member."

George Gifford (*A short Reply unto...Henry Barrow and John Greenwood,*

1591, 17) also says that Bolton was an elder in the "secret church," as does John Robinson in his *Justification of Separation* (*Works*, 1851, II. 57). The omission of Bolton's name from the Fitz paper No. 3 probably means that he had been excommunicated before 1571. A long controversy between William White, Puritan, and S. B. "an English Anabaptist" (printed for the first time in the present writer's *A Conscientious Objector of* 1575, 52, 59), gives a few additional facts.

White implores the Anabaptist "well to consider of the late judgement of God, upon a brother (as was thought) whose credit among the godly, whose praise in the Gospell, whose zeale & continuance in the same, whose persecution & exile for testimony therof was not much inferior to those that suffered most, & gave the greatest testymony (death excepted), who held no such errors, neither did condemne the Universal Church of Christ, nor cut him self therfrom, as you & your sect do, but acknowledged the saide Universal Church, as allso these members & parts therof ; the Church of Christ in Geneva, in Fraunce, in Germany, in Scotland, &c. ; allso in London the Italian Church, the dutch & the french, of which he was a member ; so that his greatest sinne knowne to man, & as his owne mouth did confesse not many dayes before his dolourous & daungerous end, was that, for judging & condemnyng a part of Christs Church, & but certaine members of the same, the heavy hand of God was upon him, which as wofull experience declares never left him untill his owne conscience, hart, & hand, was his owne accuser, judge, & hangman...."

The Anabaptist replies : "And as for Bolton...be this knowne unto you, he spake not to me in a yeare or allmost 2 before he dyed, and for this cause, he saide if the Queene would give him license and money he would make an army, and first go through England, and not leave a papist [alive], and so passe forward into other Countries. Then I asked him if that were according to the spirite of Christ, saying, whereas Christ came to Samaria, and thei would not receive him, when the Apostles would have called for fyer from heaven he rebuked them, and allso of the tares sowen amongst the good seede, and other such like scriptures as to the same end I alledged. Then hee spake his pleasure at that time, and after that never gave me word where he mette me. But I thanke god I have not bene nor am nor I trust thorow the help of Christ shall never be of his blouddie mynde."

These references confirm the fact of Bolton's exile in Queen Mary's days, and his association with a Separatist Church; his violence against the Papists is reflected time and again in the fierce invective of the papers produced by the Fitz congregation. So far as can be ascertained, there is no mention of him in the records of the French Church in London. As White's letter containing the reference to him is dated April 1576, his suicide must have occurred before then ; George Gifford, writing in 1591, puts it "about twenty years ago."

See below, p. 47, for further references.

JOHN NASSHE'S "ARTICLES."

Two other names, [Harry] Sparrow and [John] King, have already been observed[1] as those of men before the Council with John Browne and several Puritan ministers in 1573. If these two had been released, they were more fortunate than some of their company, for in January 1580/1, "John Nasshe, the Lordes prisoner," sent[2] to Convocation certain articles, in which he speaks with great audacity of the Bishops and the clergy, and claims they have kept some in prison 9 or 10 years. "John Nayshe" was among those released[3] from Bridewell on April 22nd, 1569, but it seems clear that he must (either before or after then) have joined Fitz's congregation. His narrative not only gives a statement of views almost identical with "The trewe markes of Christes churche," but it catalogues the deeds of persecution of which the Bishops have been guilty:

"in this your tyranye, you maynteyne and extoll them [ceremonies] above the worde of God, in that you persecute and imprison some, to the death of the faythful servaunts of the Lord, whose names here followe.

1. Randall Partrag.
2. giles fowler.
3. Thomas Bowland.
4. Mr Pattenson, preacher.
5. John Kynge.
6. Mr Fitz, preacher.
7. John Lernarde
8. and Margrett Racye
9. and the wyffe of Mr Causlen[4],

and others, all thees were godlye and zealous christians and dyed by your tyrannous imprisonment and cruell tyrannye. Theese with all their companye abhorred all false sects and Schismes, errors, herecyes, and all papistrye, and all false and fayned religion and stoode faste to Chrystes institution and holye religion to the death, those that dyed departed constant Christians, even in your persecution."

---

[1] Above, p. 30.   [2] Peel, *Cal. Sec. Parte Reg.* I. 147–52.

[3] Burrage, *Early Eng. Dissenters*, II. 12.

[4] Was Mr Causlen a minister? In this list all the men are given Christian names but the preachers, Pattenson and Fitz, who are designed "Mr." Possibly this implies that Causlen was also a preacher.

Of these nine, all but Mr Pattenson, whose appearance as a Separatist preacher has been noted[1], and Mrs Causlen are connected with Fitz's congregation, either being mentioned in the petition, or signing it.

Nasshe's articles are extremely long and valuable, but further consideration of them is deferred until the second of the State papers relating to "the privye churche" is examined, for with this it is closely connected.

"THE SEPARATIST COVENANT OF RICHARD FITZ'S CONGREGATION."

This paper is called by Mr Burrage, who prints a facsimile[2], "The Separatist Covenant of Richard Fitz's Congregation." No date is given.

It begins:

"Beyng throughly perswaded in my conscience, by the working and by the worde of the almightie, that these reliques of Antichriste be abominable before the Lorde our God. And also for that by the power and mercie, strength and goodness of the Lorde my God onelie, I am escaped from the filthynes & pollution of these detestable traditions, through the knowledge of our Lorde and saviour Jesus Christ:

And last of all, in asmuch as by the workyng also of the Lorde Jesus his holy spirite, I have joyned in prayer, and hearyng Gods worde, with those that have not yelded to this idolatrouse trash, notwithstandyng the danger for not commyng to my parysh church &c.

Therfore I come not backe agayne to the preachynges &c. of them that have receaved these markes of the Romysh beast."

Nine reasons for Separation follow, with a brief conclusion.

ITS RECURRENCE.

Under the year 1573 Strype[3] prints this very document, calling it "A Protestation of the Puritans," and stating it is endorsed in Archbishop Parker's hand with the words: "To this protestation the congregation singularly did swear, and after took the

---

[1] Above, pp. 8, 9.
[2] *Early Eng. Dissenters*, Opp. I. 90, and II. 13–15.
[3] *Parker*, II. 283–5.

Communion for ratification of their assent." In the document as printed by Strype, however, there is a striking addition. Between the nine reasons and the conclusion is a short declaration or covenant, which is identical (except for slight differences in punctuation, etc.) with the declaration made by the writer of the Separatist treatises in the *Seconde Parte of a Register*, and quoted above[1].

WAS FITZ'S A REAL CONGREGATIONAL CHURCH?

Had Mr Burrage noticed the occurrence of this paragraph in Strype's "Protestation," or known of its appearance in the "Seconde Parte of a Register" documents, his view that this Fitz paper is really a covenant would have been amply confirmed[2].

It is the existence of this covenant, together with the fact that Fitz's church is known to have elected its officers and to have exercised discipline, that gives the congregation some right to claim to be the first Congregational Church in England. This claim must now be examined.

Dexter's view was[3] that the Separatism of 1567–71 was of too episodic and sporadic a character to be called Congregational, and that the churches founded by Robert Browne had the true claim to priority. Possibly, however, Dexter's view would have been modified[4] had he known that the organization of Fitz's

---

[1] P. 23. Speculations as to the cause of the omission of the paragraph from the Fitz black letter sheet is useless.

[2] Though this, of course, undermines his contention in an earlier work [*The Church Covenant Idea*, 48] that Robert Browne's *True and Short Declaration* gives, in reference to the church established in Norwich, "the substance of the first known church covenant made in England."

[3] *Congregationalism as seen in its Literature*, 114, 5.

[4] Certainly he could not have written these words:

"It [the movement] was sporadic; it was sterile; as it had no ancestry, it left no posterity. During those years by which it ante-dated the church of Robert Browne, I can find no ripple on the sea of English thought fairly traceable to any act, or tract, or tradition, from it."

Every page below supplies the evidence for which Dexter had looked in vain.

church was as far developed as it is now seen to have been. In most movements life precedes literature, and it would be in the natural sequence of things, not only for Separatists to exist before the principles of Separation were stated, but for Congregationalism to be established in practice before its theories had been set forth in clear and definite language. No doubt this was in the mind of Dale when he claimed[1] that this was the "first regularly constituted English Congregational Church of which any record remains."

Mr Burrage's criticism[2] of this claim is pertinent, but it must be modified in the light of the evidence now brought forward. If a Congregational Church could not be formed before the

---

[1] *History of English Congregationalism,* 95.

[2] *Early Eng. Dissenters,* I. 92–3:

"In the first place, the Privy Church certainly was separatist and congregational, but it was apparently congregational by accident, so to speak, than because of the maintenance of any particular form of church polity on the part of its members. Also, as far as organization is concerned, was this Privy Church a regularly constituted English Congregational Church? This cannot be unconditionally answered in the affirmative. A regularly constituted English Congregational Church for the period before 1700, at least, was organized by means of a church covenant, but this congregation was not apparently familiar with that term, though it has been pointed out that the second printed document of the church is practically a separatist covenant. The real congregational church polity was only expressed later, and developed by slow evolution. This church has its part in that evolution. It was a pioneer congregation and undoubtedly made some advance over its predecessors, but not until later was organized the 'first regularly constituted English Congregational Church.' Richard Fitz's church was simply the earliest separatist congregation of which any considerable historical record has been preserved. Its ideal as manifested in the appeal to Queen Elizabeth appears not to have been a permanent separatist Congregationalism, but a national church movement led by the Queen herself, her princes, and ministers, to 'bryng home the people of god to the purity and truthe of the apostolycke churche,' utterly to destroy and remove all relics of Roman Catholicism, and to set up what may be described as 'the apostolycke churche.' The congregation does not appear to have tried to formulate any church polity, or to show what constituted an apostolic church. Other matters took up their attention, and it was left to Robert Browne first to outline that religious Utopia which they longed to enjoy, but had no hope to realize."

Cf. also I. 116.

fundamental Congregational principle—that a church is composed of Christians gathered out of and separated from the world —was held by every member, there was no full-blooded and living Congregationalism before Browne's books were written, or at any rate, before his "companie" was gathered in Norwich about 1580. Separatist churches that come before then were as framework and skeleton, but they had not the spirit and life. In support of this view could be urged the fact that so much of the writing of the Separatists—as *e.g.* the first Fitz paper— is merely Puritan and anti-Papist, aimed simply at corruptions and "dregs of Popery" in the church, and so little, if any, is directed against the territorial or parochial idea of the church.

HOW IT ANTICIPATED ROBERT BROWNE.

On the other hand the Separatists *did* gather themselves out of the world; they did realise[1] that where two or three were gathered together, there Christ was, and they believed God had separated them, and would be their Father. Although the Congregational principle was not so clearly defined by them as by Browne, yet it was, in practice, the basis on which their church was built—it was formed only of men and women who were devout Christians, and whose devotion to the idea that they must separate themselves from the world was able to carry them to prison and death. And when Browne's *Booke which sheweth the life and manner of all true Christians* is examined, there seem to be few points where Fitz's congregation fell short of the ideal church there described[2]:

Section 1.   "Wherefore are we called the people of God and Christians? Because that by a willing Covenant made with our God, we are under the government of God and Christe, and thereby do leade a godly and christian life.
Definition. Christians are a companie or number of beleevers, which by a willing covenant made with their God, are under the

---

[1] They even quote the words (above, p. 33).
[2] *A Booke which sheweth, ad loc.*

governement of God and Christ, and keepe his Lawes in one holie communion....

36. Howe muste the churche be first planted and gathered under one kinde of governement? First by a covenant and condicion, made on Gods behalfe. Secondlie, by a covenant and condicion made on our behalfe. Thirdlie by using the sacrament of Baptisme to seale those condiciones, and covenants....

38. What is the covenant or condicion on our behalfe ?

We must offer and give up our selves to be of the church and people of God....We must make profession, that we are his people, by submitting ourselves to his lawes and governement...."

All these conditions were duly carried out by Fitz's congregation, with the exception of the one relating to baptism as a seal of the covenant, and there, it will be remembered, the congregation, in Archbishop Parker's words, "took the Communion for ratification of their assent." As has been well said[1] of this little company, " their Congregationalism, though evident, was not systematically developed." No doubt they were not so self-conscious in forming their church as some congregations afterwards ; no doubt circumstances, especially the insistence on conformity in regard to ceremonies[2], largely caused the original separation; but equally without doubt Fitz's congregation was *in practice* a true Congregational Church.

In the light of all the evidence now existing, it must therefore be said that attempts to show that Robert Browne was much more likely than Richard Fitz and his contemporaries to have established the first congregational churches are more or less futile.

Mr Burrage, for example, makes the point[3] that as no account of the activities of the English Church at Frankfort was published before 1574 (? 1575), Fitz and his predecessors may have been unacquainted with them, while Robert Browne "must have been familiar with the record of its troubles, and, though his views on church polity evidently were not derived from that narrative, the very completeness of the organization of his own 'companie' testifies to such a probability." But John Browne, leader of a Separatist congregation in 1568, was actually a member of the

---

[1] Dr Williston Walker, Art. "Congregationalism" in Hastings, *Encyclop. of Relig. and Ethics.*

[2] Cf. Nixon to Grindal (*A parte of a register*, 30): "For before you compelled them [the ceremonies] by law, all was quiet."

[3] *Early Eng. Dissenters*, I. 116.

Frankfort church and took an active part in its affairs[1]. For the purpose of church organization in 1568 he had first-hand knowledge of what Robert Browne could only have gathered at secondhand from persons concerned, or from the printed record.

Again, "a certaine brother, a mynister," sent from Geneva about this time[2] a letter exhorting the Separatists to go forward with the work they had begun. He tells them that

" to abide in the assemblies of these Bishops, which do labour to stay you,...is with them to consent against the expresse building of the Apostles and Martirs, which you have seene and lived in, and whereunto you your selves were labouring and travailing, and out of the which they have cast you:...Weigh then that to receave the Sacraments and heare their prechings with them is to encourage and to alow and agree to them....Therfore it is verie expedient to begin the worke of buildinge in an other place, folowing the example of the erection of the Apostles, leaving these mens sermons and preachings as those that turne you to the purpose of themselves, and by which you are compelled in this confusion, wherin papists and Lutherans are mingled together to the hindrance of the pure and perfect example, to separate yourselves that your building...may...go forward...."

Or, in another place:

"Seeing that God hath given you the priviledge to build and to choose mynisters, elders, and deacons, and to refuse a false uniformitie"

it is not

"a sufficient discharge to remaine in open and manifest impurity and deformation, because the magistrats stay you."

"*Because the magistrats stay you*"! Here is the very accent, and almost the very words[3] of Robert Browne's *Treatise of reformation without tarying for anie, and of the wickednesse of those Preachers, which will not reforme till the Magistrate commande or compell them.*

---

[1] Above, p. 29.

[2] Peel, *Cal. Sec. Parte Register*, I. 62–3. The author is unknown, and the letter undated, but, as it speaks of Bonner as if still alive, it must be put before September 1569.

[3] Cf. also Christopher Colman's words concerning the place of the magistrate in the Church: "It is good for rulers to be in the church, and the chief thereof ; but not above, for that belongeth to Christ" [above, p. 9]. There is nothing clearer or more emphatic in Browne's writings concerning the relation of the Prince to the Church.

THE PERSISTENCE OF THE COVENANT.

Neither was the church so ephemeral as Dexter believed, especially if the persistence of the covenant be an indication. That covenant appears in a Separatist declaration previous to 1571 (for in John Browne's reply thereto Fitz is spoken of as still alive); it is given (rightly or wrongly) by Strype under 1573, and it occurs eight years later in two petitions to Convocation, sent by prisoners who belonged to this or a kindred congregation. In Feb. 1580/1 William Drewett[1] [Dreuit] notifies Convocation[2] that on Feb. 3 he had been sent to Newgate "for not consentinge to the additions and filthye ceremonyes of Antichryste, and the Romish Remnantes which is that stingginge tayle of that most cursed serpent which hath made all nations to drincke of the wyne of the cuppe of wrathe of her fornication."

Praying that the nation "maye bee released of this Romishe bondag," he says: "Yet had I rather dye in the Lordes trueth for my salvation then to live in the world with dissimulation and be confounded." Then follows immediately the familiar covenant "I have joyned my self to the true dispersed church of Chryste, etc."

To the second document[3] some reference has already[4] been made. It is headed

"Articles sent to the Bishops and Cleargye in the convocation house....From the Marshalsye by John Nasshe the Lordes prisoner 1580 Januarye."

After a violent attack on corruptions in the Church[5], and an inditement of the tyranny of the Bishops in persecuting to the death nine of the Lord's servants and keeping others nine or ten years in prison (which even "bloudye Bonner" would not do), the account goes on:

---

[1] It is perhaps worth noting that a *Thomas Drewet* is given in the Preface of the Barrowist *True Confession* (1596) as one of 24 who had perished in prison before 1593 [see Burrage, *Early Eng. Dissenters*, I. 153].

[2] Peel, *Cal. Sec. Parte Reg.* I. 152–3.

[3] *Ibid.* I. 147–52. [4] Above, pp. 36, 37.

[5] In objecting to the appointment of vicars &c. "without consent of the congregation or parishioners," Nasshe strikes another Congregational note: "this is a horrible error, for everye minister ought to have the consent and love of their congregation, and well knowene of them to bee a faythfull man, and a godlye, &c...."

"Theese and suche like Christians doo you imprison and impoverish all you can, all that wyll not yeeld to your dissimulation; you have had, at the least a thowsand persons in this citye of London, that were well bent and godlye minded, yea, and verye zealouslye goynge forwarde in the Lordes true religion, and had joyned their hartes and handes to the sincere worshippinge of God."

If it be true that at one time at least a thousand in London had "joyned their hartes and handes," then it becomes very probable that other congregations share with that of Richard Fitz the claim to priority in being the first Congregational Church. Is there any ground for thinking Nasshe's estimate is correct?

THE NUMBER OF THE SEPARATISTS.

Note, in the first place, that Nasshe admits that many of the thousand have fallen away; "theese have you most wickedlye plucked back agayne into your dissimulation and hypocrisye, and now are they with you become bondmen of men and slaves of Sathan, and as dogges turned to their owne vomitt agayne in turninge to the filthye myer of popishe ceremonyes and mens traditions, from which they were once freed, and are altogether become neuters...."

This falling away is confirmed by the words of Robert Harrison[1], yet it is worth noting that just at the time Nasshe

---

[1] *A Little Treatise uppon the first verse of the* 122 *Psalm*, D. 2 recto.

"Some...have been dismayed and offended, beholding the wayward foot steppes of divers which have gone before, even in the righte pathe, though not with steadie foote, but have slipped, halted, & falne in the waye by committing some thinge which have displeased the Lorde, *as sometime in the chiefe Citie of England, there were manie which withdrewe themselves from this spirituall bondage mentioned.* But some onelie making conscience at the Cappe & Surplesse, and therein stoode all their religion. Some entring that waye, despised all other, but pitied them not in the bowelles of compassion, that they might be brought unto the trueth, but were proude in their owne conceyte. Moste of them also ignoraunt howe they should come to the ende, or yet to the middest of the waye which they had entred, neyther being humble in seeking out the same, but thinking rather that they knew all things. *Therfore when they were tried & weighed manie were found too light, and their miscarying of the Lords Arke, and the judgement which fell upon some of them, as sore as did upon Uzzah, discouraged manie, & weakned their hands. So by their untowardness they caused the savour of the Lords work to stink in the nostrils of the people.*"

was lamenting the turning back of his brethren, Harrison and Browne were gathering their "companie" in Norwich, and so re-establishing the cause the decay of which the prisoner was mourning.

But if the thousand had greatly diminished by 1581, is there any sign that so many had joined themselves together ten years previously? With Nasshe's estimate the following numbers must be compared[1]. The Spanish Ambassador mentions gatherings of 150 and 400, and is told by a well-informed Catholic that there are 5000 in the city altogether. Stowe, in his list of meeting places, gives the numbers present at two only, and they were 60 and 120. More than 100 gathered in the Plumbers' Hall, and 77 in the goldsmith's house. The Separatist's letter to Knox says that "many a hundred…joined all with one heart and mind to serve God…." Grindal gives 200 as the total number in 1568, and this comparatively small figure is supported by the tone of most of the Separatist documents. Even though John Browne speaks of four or five churches divided one from another, he gives the impression that the number altogether was but small. Indeed, he distinctly refers to "the *small congregation* that is gathered together in this city," and blames the seceders for "the dissolving or breaking up of *this litle vineyeard or Church of God*." The estimation and confirmation of numbers is always difficult[2], but it is quite possible that at the beginning of the movement, when many Puritans would join in, as many as a thousand might have been adherents. But as soon as it became apparent to many that Separation would involve not only persecution, but also prolonged antagonism to civil and ecclesiastical authorities, their connexion with the movement would cease, and probably the true Separatists, convinced and conscientious men and women, would be confined to the four or five churches mentioned by Browne, all of them small, and their total membership probably little more than 200.

[1] All drawn from the text above.

[2] Witness Sir Walter Ralegh's guess (in the Parliament of 1593), that there were 20,000 Brownists in England.

DEGREES OF SEPARATION.

It is uncertain how far some of these other churches share with Fitz's the right to be called congregational churches. Probably some of them were Separatist only by accident and circumstance, while others had a definite Congregational organization and polity. There were no doubt differences of opinion between them concerning meeting in secret, and attending the services of Puritan preachers and parish churches generally. Considering the many congregations of whose existence there is undoubted proof[1], and remembering the suggestion of others in the names of Pattenson, Coleman, and Causlen, it will be evident that there is abundant room for many varieties of opinion and organization between the Plumbers' Hall congregation on the one hand and Richard Fitz's on the other, John Browne's, perhaps, coming about midway between. Some men were carried along with the development of the movement, and Thomas Bowlande, first a leader of the Plumbers' Hall congregation, died as a deacon of Fitz's church. At the same time John Bolton moved in the opposite direction.

Of course, many of the congregations mentioned may be one and the same—Mr Pattenson, for example, may have been a preacher in Fitz's church and not have had a congregation of his own. But when every allowance has been made for this possibility, it seems certain that, at the very least, there were the four or five churches to which John Browne refers, perhaps meeting in the different places mentioned in Stowe's catalogue.

These play a real part in the evolution of Puritanism into Congregationalism, and some of them were probably as much Congregational churches as was Richard Fitz's.

LATER BROWNISTS (AND THEIR OPPONENTS) PLACE THEIR ORIGIN IN FITZ'S TIME.

For it has to be recognised, not only that the covenant used by these churches persisted for many years, but that the memory of them, especially of Fitz's, did likewise, and on occasion

[1] See the summary above, p. 26, and the Fitz congregation in addition.

Brownists themselves trace the beginning of their movement, not to Robert Browne, but to Richard Fitz. Thus, in Miles Micklebound's *Mr Henry Barrowes Platforme*[1] Desiderius asks Miles why the sect was called Brownist. Told of Robert Browne, he asked if none wrote for the cause before Browne, and receives the reply:

"Yea, verily. The Prophets, Apostles, and Evangelists...many of the Martyrs....Also, in the dayes of Queen Elizabeth, there was a separated Church, wherof Mr Fitz was Pastor, that professed and practised that cause before Mr Browne wrote for it."

The opponents of the Brownists also looked to Fitz's church for the origin of Brownism, but they called Bolton, the elder who committed suicide, the "first founder of Separation[2]." Thus Thomas Rogers[3], writing in 1607, refers to Bolton as "he that first hatched that sect in England which afterward was termed Brownism." In Ainsworth's reference[4] to the Church, he mentions that both Gifford and Bernard have called Bolton "the first brocher of this way," and points out that he "was but a ruling Elder."

FITZ'S CONGREGATION, THE FIRST CONGREGATIONAL CHURCH.

As the next generation of Brownists and their opponents alike seem to have connected the development under Robert Browne with the earlier movement, it seems that there is no valid reason for moderns to deny to Fitz's congregation, and probably to others contemporary with it, the title of "the first Congregational Churches."

[1] Published in 1611 (not 1593, as Dale), I. 7 verso.
[2] This is Thomas Drakes's phrase (in *Ten Counter-Demands Propounded.* See Burrage, *Early Eng. Dissenters*, II. 140).
[3] *The Catholic Doctrine of the Church of England* (Parker Soc. reprint, 142).
[4] Above, pp. 34-5, where Robinson's reference to the congregation is also mentioned.

THE NAME BROWNISTS.

Is it possible that the Brownists were named after John rather than Robert? The answer, in spite of Stowe's reference to "Brownings" in 1568, must be in the negative. Not only is there no other mention of "Brownings" or "Brownists" before the publication of Robert's books in 1582, but in the discussions that arose concerning the name (which was greatly disliked and frequently repudiated by the early Separatists) it is on every occasion linked with Robert. To take but one example, chosen because it suggests that the writer knew of Separatist activity before 1582. Writing in 1617, J. Dayrell in *A Treatise of the Church, written against them of the Separation, commonly called Brownists,* says[1]:

"Your seperation is as auncient as Browne, who first caused, or at least greatly furthered that separation and schisme from our Church: whereupon you are called Brownists."

The name was employed as early as 1587 (possibly earlier), and Bredwell uses it, certainly referring to Robert, in *The Rasing of the Foundations of Brownisme* in 1588.

That the name did not secure general acceptance immediately is illustrated in Richard Harvey's *A Theological Discourse of the Lamb of God* (1590), where, speaking of those that advocate "equality," he says[2]:

"as it appeareth already by some they cal Brownists, or Downists, and Downings, or such men of plucking downe both great and litle hils...."

[1] 151.   [2] 168.

INDEX

www.ingramcontent.com/pod-product-compliance
Ingram Content Group UK Ltd.
Pitfield, Milton Keynes, MK11 3LW, UK
UKHW042150280225
455719UK00001B/234